Vision Board
Clip Art Book
for Black Women

Our special gift for you!

In appreciation of your recent purchase, We would like to extend our heartfelt thanks by offering you three complimentary bonuses.

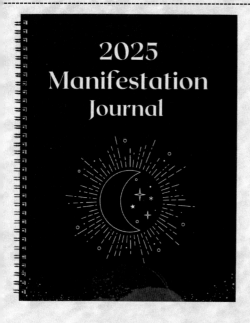

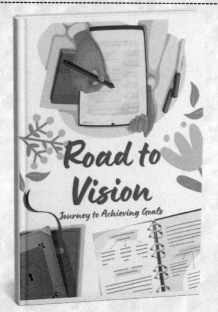

2025 Manifestation Journal for attracting goals, it will also help you visualize your vision and manifest your wishes.

70+ Positive Affirmation Cards, powerful messages for Yourself, you can use for Vision Board, Gift, Journaling, scrapbooking, And many more

Discover "Road to Vision," your creative guide to achieving your goals and dreams. This workbook includes fun and unique exercises that help you define your vision and build an inspiring action plan.

SCAN ME

Or go to:

https://payhip.com/b/6Vosb

: awesome_awareness2023   ♪ : @awesome_awareness   ✉ : awesomeawareness2023@gmail.com

What is a Vision Board and What Does it Do?

A vision board is a visual representation of one's goals, dreams, and aspirations created by arranging images, words, and symbols reflecting these desires. It acts as a compass, aligning actions with intentions, and is rooted in the law of attraction, suggesting that visualizing goals can aid in their manifestation. Key functions include clarifying goals, promoting visualization, providing focus and motivation, inspiring positive thinking, encouraging action and accountability, and fostering personal expression and creativity. However, it's essential to remember that a vision board is a supplementary tool to actions and plans, and regular updates are crucial to staying aligned with evolving goals.

Vision Board Ideas

Vision board ideas encompass various aspects of life, such as career, personal growth, health, travel, achievements, financial abundance, hobbies, relationships, philanthropy, and personal values. These ideas involve incorporating images and words representing different goals and desires. Always prioritize personal resonance when selecting images and words.

Getting Started with Your Vision Board
Follow this step-by-step guide:

- **Set Your Intentions:** Reflect on your goals across various life areas to clarify your vision.
- **Gather Your Materials:** Assemble the materials you need for your vision board, (Use this vision board clip art book).
- **Create a Theme:** Select a central theme or focus to maintain coherence.
- **Arrange and Design:** Organize images and words on your board or canvas to make it visually appealing and inspiring.
- **Add Personal Touches:** Customize your board with personal photos, affirmations, and creative elements.
- **Display Your Vision Board:** Place it where you'll see it regularly.
- **Journal About Your Vision Board:** Use journaling to reflect on your goals and motivations.
- **Take Action:** Remember that your vision board is a tool to support your goals, but you must take practical steps toward your aspirations.
- **Review and Update:** Periodically evaluate your progress, celebrate achievements, and update your vision board to align with evolving goals.

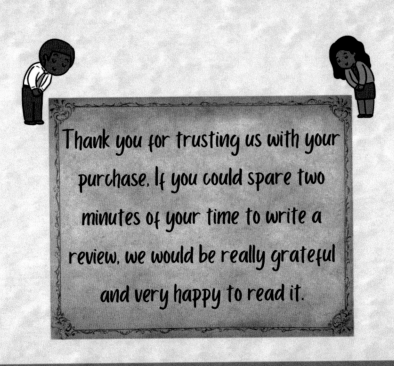

Thank you for trusting us with your purchase. If you could spare two minutes of your time to write a review, we would be really grateful and very happy to read it.

2025
I AM
READY

**NEW YEAR,
NEW MINDSET,
NEW GOALS,
NEW ADVENTURES,
NEW RESULTS.
AND
A FRESH PERSPECTIVE.**

Merry Christmas

Every year you make a resolution to change yourself THIS YEAR Make a Resolution to be YOURSELF

The New Year is a chance to write a new chapter in your life story

it's okay to feel your feelings

love yourself

BELIEVE IN YOURSELF

I Love Myself First

I ♥ ME !

YOU ARE EN♥UGH
DON'T FORGET THAT

I am worthy of love and respect just as I am

YOU ARE ★
Special

BELIEVE
YOU CAN

Be Free
my Darling

HONEY, YOUR SOUL IS GOLDEN

Self love

MINIMUM
LOW
MEDIUM
HIGH
MAXIMUM
SELF ESTEEM

Together We Can!

Happiness Is Being With The People You Love And Creating Beautiful Memories Together

I LOVE US

LOVE

Love You Forever

Let's Grow Together

I Am Engaged

DATE NIGHT

Marriage Is The
Art Of Weaving
Two Unique Souls
Into One
Beautiful Tapestry

A happy Marriage Is
A Refuge In The Storm Of Life

Certificate of Marriage

This Certifies that

_____ and _____

were united in marriage on this day.

This ceremony was witnessed and celebrated by

_____ and _____

MY BABY IS A SOURCE OF JOY AND HAPPINESS IN MY LIFE

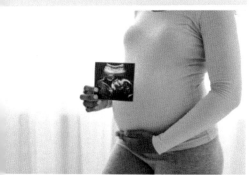

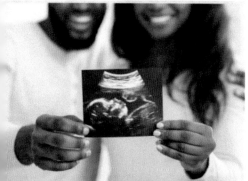

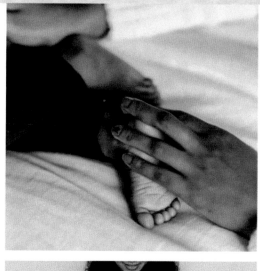

MY BODY IS Perfectly Designed for this Miraculous Journey of Pregnancy

I am Grateful For the Gift of New Life Growing Within Me

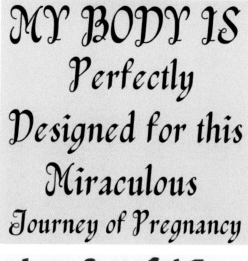

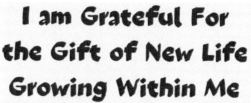

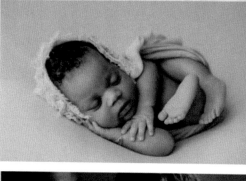

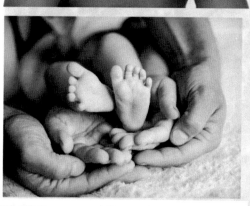

Father
Mother
Daughter
Son
Brother
Sister
Grandma
Grandpa

I am Proud Of My Family, And They Are Proud Of Me

Family

MORE FAMILY TIME

BEST FRIENDS FOREVER

Every day, I meet Incredible Individuals Who Become Friends

FRIENDS
Harder to find
IMPOSSIBLE
to forget

Better Friendship

LOVE GIVE LIFE MONEY FOOD
FRIENDSHIP HUMANITARIAN
FRIENDSHIP LEISURE HAPPINESS UNITY SUCCESS TEAMWORK COOPERATION SOCIAL FREEDOM
FRIENDSHIP
SUCCESS TEAMWORK COOPERATION SOCIAL FREEDOM PARTNER FAMILY
WORK
FRIENDSHIP HUMA
LOVE LOVE SUPPORT COMM
SUPPORT
GIVING
UNITY LIFE COMMUNITY

A faithful
FRIEND
LOVES to
the End

I Effortlessly Attract Amazing New Friends Into My Life

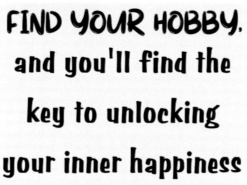

FIND YOUR HOBBY,
and you'll find the key to unlocking your inner happiness

what's your Hobby?

MY FAVORITE HOBBIES

SUBSCRIPTION BOXES

HAND ·MADE·

Poetry

Architecture

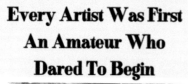

ART

CINEMA

Every Artist Was First An Amateur Who Dared To Begin

Creativity is
The Bridge
between imagination
and reality

Art
is The Journey of
a Free Soul

Sculpture

The notes of music are the ink of the heart

Gospel

DJ R&B

Pop JAZZ

HIP HOP Reggae

LET'S Dance

aFRobEat SOUL music

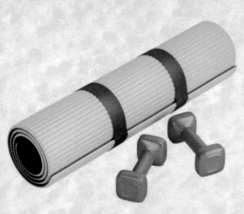

ENERGETIC

Get To The GYM

DO MORE CARDIO

FOCUS

I prioritize my health and well-being by consistently taking my Nutritional Supplements

I am Wealthy, Healthy And Happy

My Health IS My Wealth

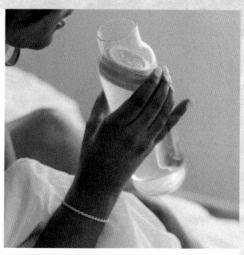

Drinking Water is Like giving Your Body a Refreshing Hug From The Inside

YOU DECIDE :(:

The 4 Pillars of Health

Vitamins   Minerals   Herbal Medicine

Dietary Supplements

Essential Fatty Acids   Amino Acids and Proteins

 Nutrition

 Exercise

 Relaxation

Eat well live well be well

Happiness is sleeping like a baby

 Sleep

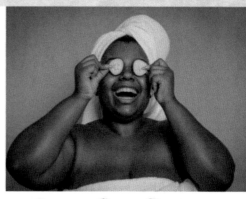

RELAX

medikate

DIARY

me time

Just Me

I AM ENOUGH

I am safe

TAKE time for your SELF

Selfcare IS NOT SELFISH

do what makes you happy

SELF-CARE

SELF CARE is a PRIORITY

I am Beayiful

Beauty is The Reflection Of Your Inner Kindness

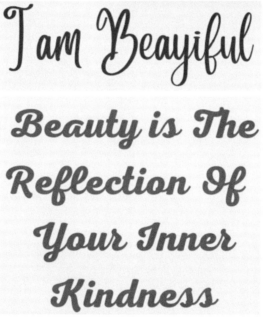

A woman's Beauty
is like a
Fine Wine
it gets
Better With Time

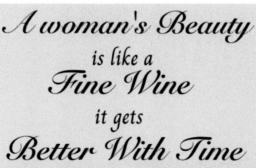
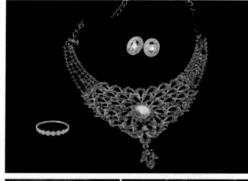

PODCAST
LIVE
STREAMING

You Have a Message To Share

do it for you

Be Bold

Follow Your dreams

YOUR LIFE HAS A PURPOSE.
YOUR STORY IS IMPORTANT.
YOUR DREAMS COUNT.
YOUR VOICE MATTERS.
YOU WERE BORN TO MAKE
AN IMPACT

Be brave enough to live the life of your dreams according to your vision and purpose, instead of the expectations and opinions of others

The purpose of life is a life of purpose.

Decide what you really want

WHAT'S YOUR PURPOSE?

decision making
planning
risk leader strategy cost

Stay PRESENT

Creating The Life Of My Dreams

I can and I will

good ♡ things take time

DO IT!
☑ NOW
☐ LATER

It's not About Having Time, It's About Making Time

I have all The time I need

TIME -IS- MONEY

I Will Make Time For Me

RISE AND SHINE

Early to bed and early to rise makes a PERSON healthy, wealthy and wise.

Discipline
Prioritize
Optimize
ORGANIZATION
Productivity

Time is the currency of achievement; spend it wisely

Balance

.9 58

January

SYSTEM
TOOLS
EFFECTIVENESS   SCOPE
PRODUCTIVITY   ORGANIZE
TIME   EFFECIENCY
MANAGEMENT
PROCESS   METHOD
SCHEDULING   PLANNING
PROJECT   CONTROL   TASKS
PRIORITIES   BUSINESS

I AM A STUDENT OF LIFE

In The World Of Education, I am The Artist Painting My Future With Wisdom

LANGUAGE

LEARNING NEVER ENDS

ONE step AT A TIME You'll GET THERE

note to self: DO NOT QUIT

WORK HARD   DREAM BIG   STAY POSITIVE

WORK SMARTER NOT HARDER

EVERY ACCOMPLISHMENT STARTS WITH THE DECISION TO TRY.

CHIEF EXECUTIVE OFFICER

Entrepreneur

Career Success
Work for Cause, not for Applause

PAY YOURSELF FIRST

Budget Reporting Controlling Control Strategic Plan Finance Balance Revenue Forecast

Become A Millionaire

OPEN

NEW BUSINESS

Debt Free
Just Ahead

DEBT

I Choose To Live A Rich And Full Life

Many Come To Me Easily And Effortlessly

My Paycheck Grows

WINNER

Invest IN YOURSELF

FINANCIAL FREEDOM

SAVING

PASSIVE INCOME

PASSION

I Attract Wealth
I am A Wealth Magnet

GOLD

WEALTH

Privileged

Abundance

- **Abundance Flows In**
- **Money is My Friend**
- My Earnings Multiply
- Prosperity Is My Birthright
- I am Financially Empowered

LUXURY

MOVING DAY

Every day, I am one step closer to living in my DREAM HOME

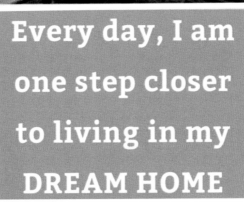

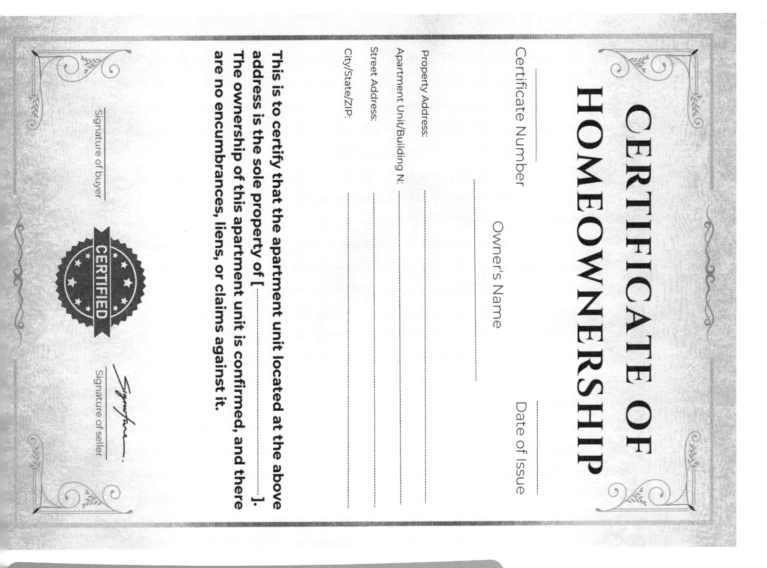

CERTIFICATE OF HOMEOWNERSHIP

Certificate Number

Owner's Name

Date of Issue

Property Address:

Apartment Unit/Building N:

Street Address:

City/State/ZIP:

This is to certify that the apartment unit located at the above address is the sole property of [_____]. The ownership of this apartment unit is confirmed, and there are no encumbrances, liens, or claims against it.

Signature of buyer

CERTIFIED

Signature of seller

Train Ticket

PASSENGER

NUMBER
LD-5647326

TIME

PLATFORM 25

SEAT 17A

PRICE

FROM

TO

TRAIN 4253

CLASS
FIRST CLASS

Train Ticket

PASSENGER

NUMBER
LD-5647326

TIME

PLATFORM 25

SEAT 17A

PREMIUM

VIP ★ TICKET ★

Exclusive People Only

THE UNIVERSAL BANK OF ABUNDANCE

Check No. _____

Date | D D | M M | Y Y Y Y |

$ _____

PAY TO THE
ORDER OF _____

THE SUM OF _____ DOLLARS

MEMO _____

AUTHORIZED
SIGNATURE _____

A1234 - 556789012345 - 0123

FIRST CLASS — BOARDING PASS

✈ ORIGIN

Name | Flight | Group | Seat

Airport | Gate | Date / Time

✈ DESTINATION

Airport | Gate | Date / Time

BOARDING PASS

Name

Flight | Seat

Date / Time

GOLD MEMBER
Unlimited Access

VIP
Members ONLY

Name :

ID : 7150-3492-0533

Bank of Abundance

PLATINUM
Credit Card

4275 3156 0372 5493

01 / 30

Manfested on: _____

Endorsement - Signature or Stamp

This check is for the sole purpose of manifesting your desires. NOT FOR deposit into a bank or financial institution

FIRST CLASS

have fun!

CHOOSE HAPPINESS DAILY

Enjoy Every Moment

Enjoyment is my priority

I FIND JOY IN THE SIMPLE PLEASURES OF LIFE

LIVE LIFE IN FULL BLOOM

Smile

Happy Motivated Enjoy

travel more

Discover

Adventure ahead

VACATION

Reading
is the passport to
inner worlds

Writing
Is Key To Unlocking
The Doors Of Your
imagination

I ♥ BOOKS

FREEDOM

EQUALITY

Safe Space

RESPECT ❤ DIFFERENCE

GIVE RESPECT

EARN RESPECT

CREATED EQUAL

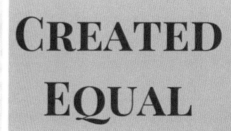

FREEDOM OF SPEECH

MY PETS

My goal in life is to be as good of a person my dog already thinks I am.

PET FRIENDLY

Pets Leave Paw Prints in our hearts

Pets teach us the true meaning Of Unconditional Love

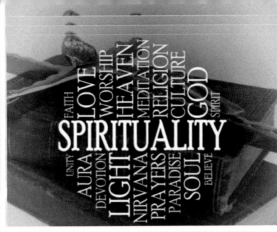

SPIRITUALITY

FAITH LOVE WORSHIP HEAVEN MEDITATION RELIGION CULTURE GOD SPIRIT UNITY AURA DEVOTION LIGHT NIRVANA PRAYERS PARADISE SOUL BELIEVE

Christianity

NAMASTE

AWAKENING

Hinduism

AWARENESS

Judaism

Angel

Religion
Energy
Miracles
Believe
The Light
Goodness
Higher Self
Divine Feminine

Islam

Prayer

BE
AWARE

Buddhism

Aries

Taurus

Gemini

Cancer

Leo

Virgo

Libra

Scorpio

Sagittarius

Capricorn

Aquarius

Pisces

How to write and use a (Letter to Your Future Self)

You can utilize this letter in a couple of ways: pin it up on your vision board to serve as a constant reminder of your goals and aspirations.
Alternatively, consider sending it to your future self.

To do so, specify the time you'd like to unseal the letter—whether it's one year from now or two years in the future—and inscribe that date in the designated spot.
Then, fill in the following sections based on your current circumstances:

Write here your current social, professional, and educational status, or all of them combined.

Write here four things that you're currently thankful for in your daily life.

Write here four skills, talents, or virtues that you admire in yourself.

Write here four behaviors or facets of your personality that you're aiming to alter.

Write here four objectives you're determined to achieve by the specified date when you open this letter.

Letter To My Future Self

On: / /20

DEAR FUTURE SELF

I hope this letter finds you happy and healthy.
As I sit here and put these words to paper, I currently _____ a high school student.
harboring dreams and aspirations that I aspire to fulfill in the days ahead.

In my daily life, I am consistently overwhelmed with a profound sense of gratitude for a multitude of things, including:

I'm grateful for the beautiful sunrise I watched

1.
2.
3.
4.

Furthermore, a sense of pride wells up within me due to the various qualities, abilities, and virtues that I possess, namely:

I am not afraid to be HONEST with myself and others.

1.
2.
3.
4.

However, I acknowledge that there are certain aspects of my personality and life that I wish to alter, and these encompass:

STOP being lazy and procrastinating

1.
2.
3.
4.

And finally, While you peruse this message, my hope is that you've successfully reached some of your goals outlined below:

1. I want to achieve a healthier lifestyle by exercising regularly and maintaining a balanced diet

1.
2.
3.
4.

No matter the results you're currently achieving, I'm confident that you've exerted your utmost effort to arrive at this point.
Remember that life is an expedition, and the paramount aspect of this journey is relishing it.
Remind yourself that I have faith in your abilities, knowing that you possess the potential for remarkable accomplishments. Continue to challenge yourself, foster personal growth, take risks, stay true to who you are, and never relinquish your dreams. I love you.
Sincerely,

YOUR PAST SELF.

Letter To My Future Self

On: ..../......./20.........

DEAR FUTURE SELF

I hope this letter finds you happy and healthy.
As I sit here and put these words to paper, I currently ....,
harboring dreams and aspirations that I aspire to fulfill in the days ahead.

In my daily life, I am consistently overwhelmed with a profound sense of gratitude for a multitude of things, including:

1. ....
2. ....
3. ....
4. ....

Furthermore, a sense of pride wells up within me due to the various qualities, abilities, and skills that I possess, namely:

1. ....
2. ....
3. ....
4. ....

However, I acknowledge that there are certain aspects of my personality and life that I wish to alter, and these encompass:

1. ....
2. ....
3. ....
4. ....

And finally, While you peruse this message, my hope is that you've successfully reached some of your goals outlined below:

1. ....
2. ....
3. ....
4. ....

No matter the results you're currently achieving, I'm confident that you've exerted your utmost effort to arrive at this point.
Remember that life is an expedition, and the paramount aspect of this journey is relishing it.
So, Remind yourself that I have faith in your abilities, knowing that you possess the potential for remarkable accomplishments. Continue to challenge yourself, foster personal growth, take risks, stay true to who you are, and never relinquish your dreams. I love you.
Sincerely,

YOUR PAST SELF,

A A A A A B B B B B C C C C

D D D D D E E E E E F F F F

G G G G G H H H H H I I I I

J J J J J K K K K K L L L L

M M M M M N N N N N O O

O O O P P P P P Q Q Q Q Q R R

R R R S S S S S T T T T T U U

U U U V V V V W W W W W

X X X X X Y Y Y Y Y Z Z Z Z

a a a a a b b b b b c c

c c c d d d d d d e e e

e f f f f f f g g g g g h

h h h h i i i i i i i j j j

j j k k k k k l l l l l

m m m m m m n n n n n

o o o o o p p p p p q q

q q q s s s s s s t t t t

t u u u u u u v v v v v

w w w w w w x x x x

x z z z z z

1 1 1 1 2 2 2 2 3 3 3 3 4 4 4

5 5 5 5 6 6 6 7 7 7 8 8 8

9 9 9 0 0 0 $ $ £ £ € €

* * ! ! ? ? % % , ,

; ; : : . . & & @ @

µ µ µ § § § à à ç ç ( ) = = + +

.. .. ´ ´ ” ” o o

— — - -

^ ^ / / < < > > ♥

♥ ★ ★ ✦ ✦ ✸

✴ ✴ ☾ ☾ ☾

Made in the USA
Las Vegas, NV
29 November 2024

12856679R00048